Books by Stephen Sandy

POEMS

PROSE

Thanksgiving Over the Water

Stephen Sandy *POEMS*

Thanksgiving Over

the Water

ALFRED A. KNOPF

NEW YORK 1992

Copyright © 1992 by Stephen Sandy

Some of the poems in this collection were originally published in:

American Poetry Review: "The Beachcomber"
The Atlantic: "Earth Day Story," "Gulf Memo," "Mother's Day"
Boulevard: "Trifid"
Grand Street: "To An Elder"
Harvard Magazine: "Around Our Table"
Michigan Quarterly Review: "The Tack," "Walking from Grasmere"
Mudfish: "Jade," "Poet in New York"
The New Yorker: "Abandoned Houses South of Stafford"
The Paris Review: "Great Plains Dooryard"
Pembroke Magazine: "To An Elder" (As "For A. R. Ammons")
Salmagundi: "Fort Burial," "Place and Fame"
Southern Poetry Review: "Zebra Skins"
Southwest Review: "Father and the Minneapolis Chacmoo!"

Poets for Life, Seventy-Six Poets Respond to AIDS, Crown Publishers, 1989;
    Persea Books,1992: "The Second Law"

Some of these poems appeared in *To A Mantis,* and
    The Epoch, limited editions published by Plinth Press.

The author is grateful to the National Endowment for the Arts and to the Vermont Council on the Arts, whose fellowships gave time to complete a number of these poems. He is grateful as well to Harriet Barlow and Blue Mountain Center for timely assistance, and to the editors of the magazines listed above.

Library of Congress Cataloging-in-Publication Data

Sandy, Stephen.
    Thanksgiving over the water: poems / Stephen Sandy.—1st ed.
      p. cm.
    ISBN 0-679-41679-X
    I. Title.
PS3569.A52T47 1992
811'.54—dc20   92-52891 CIP

Manufactured in the United States of America

First Edition

For Harry Mathews *and* Georges Guy

Contents

Contents

T H R E E

One

Earth Day Story

I remember the dusty floorboards of wood in the streetcar
Of the Minneapolis Street Railway Company
And the varnished yellow banquettes of tight-knit rattan
Worn smooth by decades of passengers
The worn gleaming brass grips at the corners of the seats
And the motorman's little bell
Windows trembling in their casings as we crossed the avenue
Liberty dimes falling softly into the steel-rimmed hour glass
The gnarled hand of the motorman near.
My grandmother arranged herself against the seat
Her back as straight as a soldier's beside me
Her navy hat with velvet band
And net veil down making her head seem distant,
Her dreaming smile and the patient Roman nose,
A repose so deep; from my place
I watched her when we rode like princes
Rattling past traffic stopped on the granite cobbles
Riding downtown together, my hand in hers;
All that so much
That I love yet but feel no sadness for, that
Time crossed out like the trolley tracks taken up
Or entombed under the pliant blacktop of the modernized.

The Terrace

The pergola saves her lunch from sunstroke,
An array of salads like bouquets
On the white tablecloth,
Shrimp nesting like orange spoons
Neat in a circular maze
Of catherine wheels, on lettuce. Strung
Between the branches of a pin oak
And an intricate beetlebung
The fraying clothesline holds—
Not crying now!—the bird Ben shot,
Its white-rimmed eyes, disinterested,
Look straight ahead, like a sloth
Staring; reclining upside down, legs spread.

The gull's rapt gaze, like a sentinel's
Is wide, but blind; like someone's blouse
The bird is drying out
Till the skull comes clean and joins the wretches
On the mantel, conch and strange
Pentacle of cloves, the starfish. Beyond
The vine that seems to spill from the truss
Of heat it bears along
The pergola's eave, a ketch is
Sailing alone in a wicker of blue,
In the clarity it would espouse
Almost outside the range
Where edges count as they extend from us,

This company our hostess yet approves
Looking seaward at the shady end
Of an al fresco meal.
The white chablis and sherbet blend.
The tablecloth, flustering at
A gust of wind, flashes a monogram
And Cousin Ben in lemon trunks
Stands guard where, to the lean
Small-boned half of ham,
Pastel toothpicks pin maraschino
Cherries and squared pineapple chunks
Hard by the cadre of dark cloves
Across the knife-scored checkerboard of fat.

Beachcomber

He considered choice, which rocks among so many
He'd pick, on the shore of boulders and bare stones,
If he chose to take some, two or three more lovely
Than the lot, or simply standouts that caught his eye
For having unusual shapes.
           Off there they stood,
The couple he'd seen that morning, spiffy in matching
Madras jams and snow-white tank tops, drinking
Mineral water near the Mexican pottery,
The place mats and Noguchi lampshades, going at it;
The seeds of fear and hollow discontent
Shining and dark as black olives pouring
Across a table top, Manhattan pair
At the water's edge now, facing the horizon,
Swash and fleece of each spent wave wreathing
Their bare feet. They stood there now, crying out
To hear each other above the tumble of the surf.

When he walked by them, they fell silent; pretended
They were a pair of concrete mannequins
Propped there watching the view. Supposing he couldn't
Hear them on the wind at twenty paces, they
Started up again, moving on each other.
Flailed, accused each other; berserk, crying,
Red as if burned by feeling, raw under
Atlantic sun; wind; the overflights
Of curious dumpy herring gulls out shopping.

Soon he felt something tracking him, perhaps
A motor launch, perhaps a biplane trailing
Some message on a banner; an apprehension
From the blue, as if he had been chosen. One moment
A quaint answer came, of horsemen cantering
In the spray, a posse of ghostly heroes. And yet
He moseyed onward, checking the tideline, the stones;
And heading back in half an hour, blundered
Once more into that couple's shady business.
They shouted into the waves where the tide lapped.
He called to them (into the onshore wind,
Which shouldered his words a dozen ways), "You now,
Lay off the living well. Give a wide berth
To the dark wood of anger! Light, take care of them."
Before, he'd thought some posse might have tracked him;
He saw now what he'd heard, the cursive din
Of fly-overs by the Air National Guard
Was what it was. He turned his back. Over
His shoulder the engines droned, *you're out alone,*
To him, a man out walking, just nosing along.

Poet in New York

Enough birds for a song
 while looking at the architecture
And clearly the rain
 comes straight at you
Like Mother Teresa, making
 demands, but sweet
When you pick up the Norfolk pine
 someone dropped on the way home;
And think how very like
 Lorca New York
And living in it really, after
 all, is.
In the failing shade of the ailanthus
 in the next back garden
You play pick-up-sticks
 with catalpa pods
Or cast strange fortunes
 with goldfish bones
Mumbling an urban
 divination
Such as that you must
 sell all your worldly possessions
Committing thereby
 a kind of suicide—the taking
Of your old, tented life—
 and step bravely into
The world of default
 and the shocking

November Sunday sun:
    but you don't. It comes to you
What came to Lorca and
    you think: we,
We only are left; and smile
    in his wry, Spanish, upstate way.

The Tack

Strait in are other chambers within
chambers, the bottom of which no
one has yet reached. COLERIDGE

Pruning pine branches, lopping bittersweet June
Out back, bitten by some creature invisible
    Or just missed, this
Was down time. I rested under the inveterate
White pine, the dark shape on my arm draped blood,
Surprising crimson scarf, how soon a welt
As broad as a Mac, rising like inky dough!
    A small invasion,

Yet fear gunned through my limbs, a pinprick panic
The blood cried *run* to; then, *what have I caught,*
    What has caught me?
The odd sensation scouted through me casually
As a cancer; like a teenager high and wilding
On a spree. Inside the house then, inside a solace
Of walls, out of the unveiled threat of heat,
    Sun like a weight.

I sat there reading at the little desk
Facing the north wall; close there, dead ahead
    On the paneled wall,
The fresh gleam of a thumbtack, boss on pine,
Shone back its steely convex eye at me.
In the tack head I saw the bow window, bow seat, the plaid
Squab in the sun, all curving in sunlight, conforming
    To its circumference:

To my left, the darker hemisphere of chamber,
Like the bullseye of Arnolfini's wedding portrait,
    In shadow but gleaming
With hints of dresser and door ajar around me,
This face like anybody's in a convex mirror,
But tiny, far, a pinpoint in the shadows
Pulling me in. A self, shuffled under
    By a sudden other.

I watched the bruise mushroom. Coleridge, despairing
Because he'd fallen from his friend and turned
    From Sara; ill
And opium-numb—en route to the Siberia
Of tacky Malta—found terror, then found what
He'd hoped to find: in St. Michael's cave, the same
Chambers, the columns, the same chasm he'd
    Imagined, writing

Osorio. It was thus to his liking, those lofty wells;
So the stung pruner grew chummy with his swelling,
    What's happened here?
Unfolding to *hello, there!,* finding whatever
It was, was him now. Acceptance. The familiar;
This melting welcome, shy; reflexive; of
Such unaccounted-for increase to his
    Anatomy.

Then tender as a new baked loaf my old arm
Felt hardly part of me, bicep and bone
    Diminished under
The swelling's pillow. The beveled head of tack
No longer beamed a guttering eye; it was

The Tack

Only a tack, flush with the wood, its wire
Needling deep, parting the tense pine fiber.
    When the fly stung

It was as if a curtain might have fallen,
Snuffing life out like a milkweed the wind sends
    Scudding to dust
And generations among the weeds; or I
As quickly disappear as a pricked balloon
One moment full of it, the next a tiny scumbag
Broken, moist on the needles under a pine
    Beside the road.

I watched how in the beady thumbtack's head
I was a millimeter shy of vanishing.
    The swelling held.
No pain. All right then. The floppy discs of memory
Kept printing feedback out, once meaningful
Segues now were synapses uncoupled:
A boyhood spanking; the homeless man in the subway
    Who talked with me;

The stray connections some deerfly had dredged up
Were nothing, though I kept falling through the net
    Of now, vertiginous.
My butt, he'd cried at ten on the rumpled bed
Though no one heard, for father had put up
The razor strop; hurried outside. The hurt
Was his possession. Those stings of guilt fell through him
    Like a slow rain.

That November when I went down below
To a soiled stillness, the cold platform stood
    Unechoing, empty,
Surrendered to a slow clock. I sat on a bench
Bent on my thoughts, the unabashed abandon
Of the city, in the streets the poor on watch
As from the hillside of abandonment;
    Deserted village

Of the collective heart, center ungrieving
And forsaken. When I looked up a panhandler—
    His ragged shape
Looming against the gray fluorescent twilight
Of that limbo station—stood before me; stood
In his pants—or his pants hung around him like
A voting booth. And he was in there somewhere,
    Making choices.

The beggar began then, bowing slightly, palms
Pressed together. I gave him—money. He said,
    "Bless you, young man."
He touched his hands to his lips—for the buck I gave—
And blessed me. My nod elicited first one
Then another remark about my goodness. I shrugged.
Out of the dark the boisterous train came on
    Pushing before it

The black air of the tunnel against us. The rest
Of his life and the rest of mine were about to be
    Two different things.
Under his filthy anorak he wore
A filthy undershirt, each stitch picked out

In grime; and the flesh was stained, and dark. Again
He bowed, "God bless you," and the track below gleamed
    With oncoming light.

And Coleridge, deep in the cave, saw "crown upon crown,
A tower of crowns, the models of trees in stone."
    Nature had doubled
An infinite beauty in his fantasies.
But they were imageless; rested in darkness until
His torch gave form to them. Here was a forest,
"A bushy-branched oak, all forms of ornament
    With niches for images

Not there." Whatever he found, first found itself
In him; there were no images now. Stalactite
    To stalagmite, drip
By cold calcareous drip. No vaulted chambers,
"No saints or angels." One shaft descended hundreds
Of feet, until "the smoke of torches became
Intolerable." And he rose for air to the blue,
    The resolute day.

Down there in his corner with dignity, the tramp
Bore witness, accosted me from the homeless land
    Emerging from nowhere,
From polluted night, like one of Van Gogh's miners,
Like the coal miner up from a Pennsylvania hill
Shining the little lamp on his forehead straight
In my startled face. "Here now," I said and took
    A ten from my wallet

And handed it over. His last word died in the roar
Of the train arriving; I left him to wander, to con
    Or bless more travelers;
Yet watching the burnished thumbtack, tunnel mirror,
I caught his rushy odor still, the white wine
Of his urine; understood that blessings were; that I
Had been chosen, even as I was punctured by
    The awaited fly.

Pen Doom

Draw a deep breath,
Happy possessor of a disordered heart!
A violent dark power seeps through
What fragmentation is.

Happy possessor of a disordered heart,
Suddenly he's just there scribbling letters.
What fragmentation is
Worse than finding he's a xerox of some original?

Suddenly he's just there scribbling letters
In the simple world of visible things—
Worse than finding he's a xerox of some original.
And all he saw was what he saw

In the simple world of visible things,
Things outside like a dish of landscape or Roman coins;
And all he saw was what he saw
In the fresh software of the future.

Things outside like a dish of landscape or Roman coins
Made something after all he could pick up on
In the fresh software of the future.
Knowing a world was there before time crashed

Made something after all. He could pick up on
The bus breaking down that shivered, undressing.
Knowing a world was there before time crashed
He saw his space was about repudiation.

The bus breaking down shivered, undressing
A man raising his hat.
He saw his space was about repudiation
In the knowledge that there were others, only others,

A man raising his hat
Drawing a deep breath
In the knowledge that there were others, only others
A violent dark power seeps through.

Home Dog

Bounding among the walkers
He gladdens, wagging, happy along
The disturbed ladies lapping

Days rinsed white. Does he trot
In dreams from the morning-glory
Arbor veiling a dumpster

To the peach by the belvedere?
His red coat ripples, ripples
When he romps along this headland

Where sentinels keep watch.
Her peat-pot eyes stare out
As if from the white sphagnum

Tangle of her hair.
Loudly the woman accuses
The bedridden one, who weeps.

No one can find the hairbrush!
Calamity, calamity
Among the atolls of

Abandonment. He scampers
Happy to the cries, the odds
And ends, blue plastic bowl

Of curlers; garnets; sepia print
Of the youth, her father. The clutter
Diminishes, sinks in

The wallpaper of taupe
Roses; folds of the curtains
Listen, wait. Not bored and not

Restless the dog turns from an old
Scent; takes up a post at someone's
Feet, by someone's slippers;

Familiar faces fallen
Quiet. The steady breathing.
Nothing doing, at last.

A Bamboo Brushpot

It was for my table, to put my pencils in
While I considered a fresh way to begin,
This brushpot chance had brought my way, a coarse
Bamboo copy of a Chinese emperor's,
Minutely carved in boxwood. My bamboo showed
A mountain wall with billowing cliff that flowed
In tumult round its sides, then fell away—
Revealing a tableau of men at play.
It told of one who ruled well long ago:
Old Xie An, now seated at a low
Table; around him attendants in court dress;
All concentrating on a game of chess.

The minister would play, but he can hear
The sound of messengers, whose charioteer
Draws up his team around the bend. The horses
Neigh; the news is of vast enemy forces
Invading the Northern frontier. Xie An plays;
Deliberation rules while he surveys
His partner's options, and the partner makes
His move. The game continues. A new day wakes
The far side of the wall. News from the North:
For two days victory flew back and forth;
Now Xie An has conquered. He refrains
From looking up. At the board his hand remains
Poised for a move. Aloof alike from word
Of victory or defeat, he has not stirred.

This botched pot's crudely carved, volume and line;
Of humble pulp that won't admit the fine
Detail that pleased an emperor once, and yet
That cloud-capped game's too earnest to forget.
May he continue play beside my chair
And I, to news just made, turn a deaf ear;
Go to confusion's bleachers as to school,
Greet squalid terror with stolidity;
And the cloudy invader with such deliberate cool
As showed an old man's skeptic mastery.

Edge

As on the treadmill of a dream
The steady quarrying of time

Recedes in a dumb armada out
Of port; of sight, below the verge

Of the sea. And do not question him,
For he is azure and will linger late

At the window, dozing where the clouds
Like politicians swell and show

Ebullient profiles to the light.
From the street, through sleep, he'll hear the noise,

The unsteady beat of studied boys
On bikes, scarring the afternoon;

And the quiet thud of a kitchen knife
Slicing fat cukes for crazy brine.

Abandoned Houses South of Stafford

Although you said there wasn't time I stopped
In Yorkshire, an intruder on the cattle
Grazing; tramped those grassy aisles and halls
Of Yorevale Abbey, ramparts of disaster,
Worn lattices of absence; tawny stone
Climbing the air. And here the stripped houses,

Bare clapboards the drifting weathers scoured, dry
Barracks for nothing—even disaster absent—
Brought back those elder ruins. The half-effaced
Facades stood up in the chilly apse of April
As if hung there from little swags of cirrus
Through the blue media of cold and light.

Since you had gone, I went to look, desiring
The walk, if that was what there was, on weekends.
The rocked walls rode on the momentous soil;
In the sun some wisps of wallpaper would flutter
From an upper room's plaster-and-lath that leaned
Crazily under the stress of beam and stud,

Hung on like petals to a blossom blown.
Doorframes with fluted columns, delicate cornices,
Panes of an Adam fanlight framed the meadows;
Windows opened on cows, the eyes of cows
Opening on windows; in a pasture, houses tumbling
Like the abbey among cows grazing Yorevale field.

Glisterings off the lake downhill flickered, lapped
At gravestones leaning like the abandoned dwellings
Back in Stafford—liver-spotted marble
From Vermont, red slate, Connecticut sandstone; grass
Crowded some fallen markers laid out level
As hearthstones, lifting them so they rose like lids

Opening; while other flags descending sank
Under the radiant blank of windy sky;
Dipped below turf, thick hanks of green scrolling
Them over. I froze to see; for you had gone;
For the derelict earth was warm, and young; the doors
Framing those meadows, meadows framing those doors.

Two

Outside Tucson

In spite of the crackle-glaze scatter
Of paths among low plants
Green palo verde, blue palo verde
I could see the guide but couldn't get there

A little ride-out through the cacti
The guide herself trying to pick up the trail
She called back, *all trails lead somewhere*
Ah! or used to

Tiniest miniature lupine
Each least and farthest star
Tattered calico asters
Blue palo verde, green palo verde
Practiced renunciation

Etiquette of the trail
One
Horse length apart
Single file, quiet

The space shy and scared
Cat's claw acacia, teddybear choya, greasewood
Bristled apart
In dread of crowding

Water table sinking forty feet a year
And the seguaro:
Sixty feet, two hundred years

Outside Tucson

The one bird overhead then
A sparrowhawk, sunlight
Through tail feathers

Sun pressed my shoulder
Pressed the desert leaves
Green palo verde, blue palo verde

The succulent's motionless aggression
Tightlipped lemon silence
Twelve miles from IBM's white lawns

The hawk sailed
Making a shadow
Drift over the ground; me—
Away over the desert leaves and flowers.

Place and Fame

I

When I was eighteen and he came
To "say his poems" Robert Frost
Stayed in the memorial guest suite
Tiny wing off a great brick dorm
Decked out with shutters and cedarshakes
To look like an eighteenth-century Cape
With flowers and a knee-high picket fence
Around the dooryard, very private
And not to be approached by us.
Once each year he came, one year
He arrived three times, always by ten
In the morning, when he vanished
Into the cottage to prepare himself
For his appearance at the end of the day.
One time the master's wife revealed
That he took nothing in his retreat
But three raw eggs, always three
Raw eggs. Gently mystified
She said she thought he put them down
The toilet (shells and all) and then
He'd open up the clandestine roast
Beef sandwich stowed in his bag of poems.

2

When Noland put The Gully up
For sale he had no takers until
The National Register listed it—
The farm Frost owned for twenty years.
When a celebrity producer
Had finally bought it and made it more
Like home (in the manner of Bel Air)
It flowered in chintz; enough pillows
To bed a cast. He found this sign
At a local shop, *By All Description*
This Should Be The Place the legend read.
It was Victorian, the owner's pride
And joy, her trademark and the one
Item (Meg told me more than once)
She would never sell, no matter what.
She sold it for a hundred bucks when he
Had a replica made for her, and no one
Guessed her famous sign was a repro
Unless he happened to check the original
In the bricky foyer of The Gully.

3

Time counts, and time was counting when I once
Met Frost at Homer Noble Farm. He'd been
Through Kennedy's inauguration and was
About to go to Russia for the President.
Ann Gentry was cooking dinner for eight, and I
Was carefully coming down the steep stairs
When he appeared from his uphill studio.
Late sun reddened the famous face he wore
In front of the taut face I felt his eyes
Peered at me from. Under the open shirt
The wrestler's shoulders sloped with age to arms,
To hands, spread fingers holding in each grip
A huge uprooted head of lettuce, roots
Still shedding gobbets of earth on the step at his door.
"So you're the guest," he said, "and I don't know
Your name." I gave my name. He'd not remember,
For I'd been only a boy in a room of boys.
"I've got the salad from my garden here.
My contribution. Maybe you'll take it in to Ann."
Behind him in shade toddled John Berryman.

4

Frost ate, and when he wasn't eating, talked.
He let you know he knew about baseball.
He said he was thinking over what he'd tell
Khruschev after he'd said him "Mending Wall."
After Ann's sirloin, the salad and the wine,
After ice cream on cantaloupe and cake
We sat around the living room drinking gin
Though Frost drank glasses of rum and lemonade
With a splash of sugar, which I was appointed to bring.
Now Berryman and Frost on opposite ends
Of the swaybacked Empire sofa eyed each other
And the long upholstered void between them. "What
Ever happened," said Berryman, "anyway,
To Empson? You knew him in England did you not?"
John fixing him with a cool stare then, Frost
Hung fire, some of us thinking how Empson was
At work in England that very minute, when
At length Frost drew the hand that held his glass
Along the sofa's back toward John and looked him
In the eye and said, "some of us pass by."

5

In the noontide of his powers,
A boy's will coupled with the man's
    Achievement, he drove round town
Delivering his son's cut flowers—
Just like a pair of also-rans
    To set up (father and son)

As florists in Vermont!—
Was what folks whispered, though he was
    Just helping out he'd say
On every morning's floral jaunt
Through Bennington, Main Street abuzz
    To see the great bouquet

His Packard had become.
He did not say he drove for love,
    No more could estimate
The little, local vacuum
For letters, or the town's gossip of
    His yen for real estate.

One day a woman called
From the Catamount to him in his roadster,
    Deliveries at the side
Door!—told him, who had enthralled
London; told him, the very lodestar
    Of the countryside, astride

Their narrow valley like
The genius of the place, at peace
    And home where he was born!
He was impressed that she could strike
Home so simply. It might release
    Him from this wild, forlorn

    Routine he'd taken on,
Thinking about his place in town
    And trying to help his son.
At The Gully farm on the high lawn
He pondered. The boy was so cast down.
    What he could do, he'd done.

Zebra Skins

They threw a zebra rug, the very pelt
of a big brown-striped one tanned and lined
and the little ears still clinging at one end,
over the Steinway in the big room.
To him it was only a plush
silliness, smarmy taste in piano decor
but later, back in his room with the flies—
a troop descended from a few

clinging to their host's riding boots, escapes
to the safe pine woodlot of rafters
under the eaves, or behind the walls—he saw
how much there was to learn. Their host
the metals magnate used that room as a tack room
after riding over his property
getting some exercise after New York.
Generations of flies

stepped carefully out of their dark rooms
into the downtown of daylight and flailed
in dozens at the skylight bubble too high
for him with a fly swatter up on a chair
to swing at. But nights they descended
to lamps and he knocked them off in dozens.
The insidious buzz of their phalanxes
railed at the windows, sizzled, then

lay silent in the wastebin. At last
it was quiet enough, and he could remember
the zebra; his host's South African mine;
the languishing veldt of the haughty eland,
elephant genocide, Baluba ivory thug.
It was the estate of violence, the hung sword
over the innocent, the faithful in Nero's arena,
the insect roar, and then the stillness.

The fear of it bloomed from the placid deer,
from the blank check of their welcoming eyes
creatures of infinite simpleness, gentle affinity,
that their ingenuous patron arranged to be tamed
and fed two meals each day; and who
before he died decreed the zebra's skin
should not repeat not be removed
from his long ebony Steinway lid.

Trifid

In the building of glass, in the city's
Dutiful violence of heights
The man once blond
Enjoys the day that is his
Aroused while he works
Writing checks
And watches blue sky out his windows
And far below, the swarming highways, the busy river
Quicksilver under the light of noon.

*

Chill evening, I listen to the motor;
Switch on the headlights in the early dark.
For a time I sit in the car before going
As I wonder about the fuel running out,
And the power; cruelty
Of megawatts to birds
And maples shriveling on the hill.
Sentiment in a jar, I think; and still
I ask if I'll get through without a hitch
Before I am out in the cold
In the dark with only the dogs.
Chill evening, I listen to the motor,
I can watch my breath
And see the dogs running, crossing my lights
Like white wolves in front of me
Through the darkened neighborhood
Barking, roaming.

Trifid

*

Some doughboys are mugging for the camera
Grinning; someone
Is handing out letters randomly. Any letter
To any soldier. Fresh troops come up
To take letters. Clearly the letters
Are all from home and all counterfeit;
This filmed grouping is propaganda, serious
Footage to use Stateside. Now
The soldiers are laughing

Through tears,
Their limbs do not follow them
To the ambulance. They keep in line
Hands laid on shoulders, eye-blisters
Wrapped in bedsheet bandages.
In a shaded ward the amputees
Are smiling, smiling. Because
It tickles? They are going home? Because
They are idiots?
Smile away, Yank, beautiful boy,
Your fresh stump humming!

Twenty After

And the terrorist down by the tower must puzzle, must guess.
He connects the fuse of the unfamiliar device

He bought for a visa in the Tangiers souk
And sets the timing and takes another look

At the hourglass profile of the stack, as tall
As a merchant bank above him. He wants to call

It off, but must call home—and homebase—first;
Must stop thinking; or stop thinking the worst.

Once more he recovers his wits; he thanks
His stars it might just do the trick and thinks

How alternative ways of proceeding were duly weighed
Though he knows his scheme, while not hopeless, is flawed

Like all but one or two of the moves he has left.
At last he punches the button, which gives him a lift,

And steps with the air of a hiker into the road
Singing, "the half life within us and abroad."

Tyros

I

On the Navy base
Everyone stood in his rank
Wearing white cotton
Bellbottom trousers and white
Blouses each with one
Chevron, or half one chevron.
This was in the wind,
On parade. The wind gently
Flapped the white, slapping
Limbs randomly, flashes of
White cotton. No one
Said anything for hours
It seemed, except, "I
Have to piss" in stage whispers;
Stood at attention
First, then at parade rest, in
Bright sun, blue breeze.
The formation was broken
Fifteen minutes before noon.

2

You may remember
    when you were in boot camp pent
An Army recruit
    on deep-sink the livelong day
Of KP, old rags
    long wet in the number ten
Cans under that sink
    were white and soft as boiled rice
With maggots slowly
    afoot; from which vision of
Your little problem
    you were torn by the far-off
Bark of the head cook
    sending you to some fresh air
    under the full moon, and sleep.

3

In boot camp they were once
marched to sick bay; seated
in a scoured lobby to wait
for vaccine and a wanton
Yellow fever shot
should they be sent to Asia.

It was one more hurry-up-
and-wait line, ennui of mud
on boots, drying to powder.
And strapped to a gurney there
in the hall, on center stage,
untrousered, a man lay, prone.

The buried agenda of pain,
of power grew manifest.
The doctor was to do
his spinal tap soon now
and there, obedient, they sat
receiving this bit of training

by means of visual—and soon
audible—aids as the doctor
held up the needle, long
as a dipstick, checking it
by the strip of fluorescent light
in the hall painted neutral gray.

Dispensing with anesthetic
he went to work and eased
the needle home. The gasps
of pain grew more, tormenting
the ammoniated air,
though in modesty the man

had turned his face to the wall
away from the boys' eyes,
bug-eyed recruits who followed
orders, waiting turns
to step up, as the captain said,
step up, step up like a man.

Pledges

I

We did not speak when father drove downtown
To the movies. I dreamed of risky missions in the dark
But those night journeys were secure delight.
We followed Niven or Muni in black-and-white
Through harrowing escapades we braved together;
Ran guns past foolproof Gestapo checkpoints; rose
To virtue's challenge, freeing Maquis heros
By the truckload. Wartime, and I was ten and stayed
Up late. With chocolate rations, we sat side
By side at the old Majestic where they played
Sequined spy operas set in war-torn Europe.
I was right with him, hoping against hope
When the hero got caught by the electric eye
Detecting his revolver, which set off
A spine-jangling siren. But the man in the trenchcoat
Would toss a key back to them; it would float
Through the electric barrier's charged air
Causing the horn to sound a brief, fat blip
That caught the guards off guard; the hero slipped,
As always, through their net, to the applause
Of factory hands fresh off their shift—and us.
He'd foiled the Nazi butchers, he had played
And won, *pro patria;* he had rescued
A crucial scientist who must not fall
Into their hands, or fighter for our cause
So pure and ardent he might save us all.

That was the way: feel good about it, chosen,
Breeze through the secret mission, in danger find
Victory's bold embrace; who paid no mind
To the sluggish streets of treacherous intent;
Or tropic stronghold, desert city, blindfold
Night; under a blazon
Of old adventure, the motto, *serviam.*

2

O happy days, O happy reader of *Life*
Magazine in those palmy days of May
1968, when Paul Newman
Campaigned for McCarthy in Indiana and
Fans of the first Kennedy held Hollywood
Galas for the second, who was still
Not dead! Back in the black-and-white section

    John Crowe Ransom is feted at eighty
    Allen Tate is remarking how
    his poems are minor only in their
    brevity; Lowell gives him a gavel
    made from one of Jefferson's
    oak trees. I thumb those upbeat
    pages, the brittle photo ops
    and ancient reservations of good fun,
    the rosy kids all smiles who pile
    into the red convertible,
    whose grille seems to be smiling too.
    I flinch to think what is in store.
    There's nothing much about a war

though here, between the politics
and the poetry, is a color feature
profiling an African wildebeest.

The pack of wild dogs circles him
who stands his bit of veldt and stares
in the lavender light, woodenly propped
on his legs. It's only a matter of
muscles in rigors of shock, as the dogs
untie the gift of his intestines.
And here he lies, a carcass, half
air already. The pack slinks off.
No need to come this way again.
The ignorant bliss of the beast as it
aimlessly grazed was done; your ease
was over too, my country, smirking

Along the glossy pages of *Life!* Your day
Had come; how like the laggard on the drumhead of grassland,
Or like the tourist on a mean street, loitering,
Set up, cruising there along the shores
Of the profitable world, a place (if it
Could be gotten into shape) possessible
In the blue twilight of innocence by a country
Without a castle;—like the first little pig,
Grasping at straws in the gusts of change, of a lusty
World recovering in its hungry bastions;
Getting better; wanting its old, own way.

3

Soon the man in the khaki jacket ground
    his cigarette and put
    his index
Finger to the lips, which opened; pressed it
    against the teeth, which parted;
    pressed it all
The way, onward and down. Then the other
    fingers of the hand touched him
    chucked him
Under the chin, cupping it; closing it.
    The docile jaw closes
    on the roaming
Finger, the lips come up on the finger
    sucking, like a child sucking
    his thumb. O yes

And I ask how much love he required, this
    man who gave himself up
    so gladly
To be a gift in an exchange of gifts
    hostage for hostages with
    the mighty
Saracens. Doubtless no one told him of
    those Christians in the vast
    underground
Prisons of Moulay Ismail, the hundreds swept
    three centuries ago from
    the sea, swept
Into the sunless cellars of Meknes, far

from the salt onshore breeze;
    so many
Taken to buy respect from Louis.

The man allows him to do this for what
    seems a long time though it
    is only
A minute or two; the bound one keeps on
    doing it after the man
    has hit him
With the clenched fist of his free hand. This is
    the beginning, what happens to someone
    who is serving
Now in the whole bliss of sacrifice.
    The younger men who are
    standing there,
Who nabbed him, understand this completely, it
    makes perfect sense to them
    and they are
Going to help. No one gives tears to death
    in the country of fear-fledged
    violence.

I think when he stepped into the black
    sedan of their cruelty
    he could not
Have known how when the king scoffed at Moulay
    those tars would end their cuffed
    days serving
Mint tea—or cleaning after camels—for
    the faithful who'd bought them from
    the sultan.

A kind of hunger creeps in, the candle of pain
    burns, lights up that low
    cellar, brightens
The young faces with familial warmth.
    It is too late to make him
    an ostler,
A footman, a drudge, who needs it? A man
    is trussed with nylon, duct tape
    on eyes and
Ankles. They prod here and there. One holds
    a 45 to the man's
    lips, nestles
The barrel there until you know the mouth
    knows what it is. He nudges
    it, the jaw
Opens just wide enough to let it in.
    No one speaks. No one
    says a word.
This man, who wears a beige safari jacket,
    moves the barrel; the ring
    of men holds.
A car passes outside, above. Soon he
    removes the barrel, slowly.
    The prisoner
Has handled this well, has not shown any emotion,
    the lips closing while
    the man wipes
The barrel across the chest which heaves, breathing.
    He wipes it; touches the forehead,
    fires it.

Gulf Memo

Tell me the way to the wedding
Tell me the way to the war,
Tell me the needle you're threading
I won't raise my voice anymore.

And tell me what axe you are grinding
Where the boy on bivouac believes,
What reel you are unwinding
For the girl in her bed who grieves.

While behind a derrick's girder
He watches the sinking sun,
He asks what he'll do for murder
And what he will do for fun.

Will you read him the ways of war
His Miranda rights in sin,
Will you tell him what to ignore
When he studies your discipline?

He dozes off—but he shakes
In a dream that he is the one
Death finds abed and wakes
Just as the night is done.

Tell me what boats go ashore
Riding the oil-dimmed tide,
Red streamers and black in store
For the boy with a pain in his side.

And tell me where they are heading
Tonight; now tell me the score.
Tell me the way to their wedding
I won't raise my voice anymore.

Jade

O Jade, Jade
I went to see you, climbing the stairs of your Yankee ghetto
Tenement, and found you in the little room
Of your younger brother
Where the pecan paneling peeled from the wall, where the fake
Gold ping pong trophies of your brother
Lined up like surplus gear in an army-navy store

Jade, Jade
You stole their sugar by putting too much in their teacups
Then licking it out when they had done
Along with their bitter meaningless dregs
Serf of your own countrymen
Hoping they would not convert
Or kill you

Jade, Jade
Lying down with the scorpion and the ant
Gentle, vanquished, singing
You saved your master sergeant
Carried him out from the burning
June of Viet Nam, like Aeneas bearing his father
On his shoulders from flaming Troy

Jade, Jade
You lay with the leeches and the snake
In the night of the jungle swamp the gift of water
Deep under the dark America left behind

You sucked breath through a straw when your guards
Spewed their roses of flame over the great green leaves
You found your breath by your love

Jade, Jade
Your eyes shining with love for all men, you
Were the one who walked in from the snow and made us feel
So cold, so cold
I climb through the decaying building past curlicues
Of stale grass smoke and fresh grass smoke knit
With the wiry odor of urine, up to the last door

Jade under the roof
Of Jade, brewing a little Lapsang Soochong for us
Under the damp-crazed sagging roof
In the room with one window looking out on another roof
O Jade pouring my tea, quietly weeping for lack of sleep
Debris of toys your baby nephew strewed the floor with
Like memories of a future that will never be

Jade, Jade
Give in the going back, although the fathers
Abide with you. You did forgive me
A whiteness at the edge of the dark
I held you in my arms and you held me in your arms
There in black snow outside the North Street tenement
So thin, so thin, so thin under your thin coat.

Smoke

The kid stood at a kind of parade rest
With his back to the wall in the crowded room. Someone
Came up saying hello and he continued there
Silent, head cast down as if in sorrow.
He seemed to study the shadowy floor. It was
Not a wince he gave the other but
The slightest shrug, disdain or greeting. It was
Apparent somehow that he must not speak, was supposed
To be standing there that way, faint shawl of neon
Glowing on head and shoulder, wearing his blue
Work shirt, acid jeans and half-laced high-top shoes.
The crowd went on with Saturday night and paid
No mind; a kid on the arcing rainbow of
His one life, controlled by another, deeply
Imbibing what he was and was becoming.
The shifting light caught in a chain at his neck,
Glinting links from another world. Someone
Had given the order, someone had left him there.
He stood until a youth came up and whispered
Something; the kid went straight to one who had
Entered unseen from a side door, a short man
In a blue shirt and levi's. The kid looked down
Lighting the man's smoke for him, the one
Relieved now sat on a stool and lay his head
On the man's breast and the man embraced him there
Long and long looking out over
The kid's shoulder into the dusky lobby
Of bodies, fresh smoke scarving from his lips.

The Second Law

Beside the bed I watch
        His hindered face
The dented cheeks lifting
        And falling
Scarcely perceived, with the stoking,
        The curbed
Breathing. I hold the mug of black
        Coffee fresh
From the nurse's station heat
        Is working its
Arduous way through the glazed
        China wall

To my cold hand. Soon
        It is too hot
To hold, I put it down
        And I take
The colder hand in mine
        And I wonder

If it is taking any warmth
        From mine
Or if his chill alone
        Is oozing
Through the wall of our grip our
        Holding on. I

Stand outside the bars through which
The gaze clings
And the stubble crowning the sheet
And the jailed
Knowing, letting him, letting him
Go.

Father and the Minneapolis Chacmool

This postcard shows you gaming, eyeing four players, each
Of them you in the poker game faked with mirrors, your
Solitaire changed to the macho game of five card stud,
Your hair in the photo slicked down so neat in 1930
Eyeing your opponents, each at first appearance
A different man, each dapper as a dictator, each you.
And where will I meet you, now you have gone to the dead
    below?

Can it be? The Minneapolis Chacmool, unveiled, is fake.
That eyes-right corker I'd adored since childhood, leering
At the Chinese tomb guardians staring through the sun
In the next gallery back at him: the label notes
He has been "widely exhibited here and abroad" yet now
They know: not some recarving merely of the face
Or prosthetic limb to double for one broken off

One high noon of bloodlust revelry in elder Mexico,
But the entire sculpture, made for market, skull to toe:
An old con man craning his head over his shoulder
Like a peeping Tom—like you, father—on a chock-full beach.
The Chacmool right as rain wears latticed sandals; holds
A bowl for the priest in his lap: the red hand of the priest
Would ease his grip on the turquoise haft of the jade dirk

Father and the Minneapolis Chacmool

With spalled green blade and hold aloft the steaming slick
Heart sliced from the winning youth; and place it there;
But this one is barefoot, and his hands lie empty now,
Limp on the dusty lap, a sort of driving cap square
On the crown of his giddy head, shading a general's gaze.
They seemed so genuine we shook when they went wrong.
Old man, I wish you well; old man, I send you love.

Three

Walking from Grasmere

Running up the browsed hillsides
Over the hillocky pasture lots
Unfallen walls wove courses,
Repeating mud-hued stones
The ridged copings rhythmic there
Like the backbones of Brontosaurs

A herd where it fell
Freezing, benighted or famished, inert
Silent as the muddy sheep
That fed along the combed slope
Or sprawled, legless wool-sacks
Growing from sod. Overhead

Out of the steelwool cloud cover
Low into the spacious afternoon
Red as a redcoat a jet fighter
Gouged loud into the valley;
Out. It saturated all
With echoes from afar

Knouting the air,
A name of sound for all
That prim, enduring world.
I looked up, back, knowing
My thoughts like the stone sheep
Like that potted landscape were the past.

To a Mantis

It's as if I hear far-off cries; I turn
To the shelf
Where the mantis eggs lay, forgotten, three
Hundred eggs
From Pennsylvania in a taped box marked
Beneficial
Insects, from which one has crawled now and stands
On the lid
Wobbling and tiny in the kitchen warmth
Like a scumble
Of spider web; yet arms outstretched as if
To hold
A fly, Martian eyes peeled; this waif ready
To help
In the yard: and three hundred more inside.
Outdoors
With them now! Finding half of them dead, cooked
In my kitchen,
I spread the rest on honeysuckle, spruce,
A swale
Of sourgrass where an elm stump rotted.
Cold night
Gone by, a little band not quite dead yet
From exposure,
Small as the mosquitoes they'd save me from,
Quivers
And stretches in the small bowers, swelling
With dew,

Tottering on their posterior limbs
    Apparently
Watching some ants that carry off their dead
    Brethren
For supper. These more than underprivileged
    Lives feel
Some whiff of joy in the foolish breeze, and
    Turned now
I toward this world feel exaltation, here
    In this little
System, motherless blinkers in the wind
    Of demise.
In two days, even the living have flown
    To hiding
Or death, I do not know. O brother sun,
    Warm this
Honeysuckle; sister honeysuckle,
    Shelter,
Give honey to the mantis. O brother
    Mantis,
Grow, devour the pests; be at home, stay
    In my yard!

Those Sky Days

They have no sense of sky
They who go there to learn, no way
To make a scripture of December fields.

The field was like an endpaper stroked with pen trials
Of a book about to be sacred
Written in
With patience
Along the scored guidelines of the frost.

The stricken corn stalks whispered
Bending under snowy miters.
The strangers kept in rented rooms

When the field was filled with scrolls trembling
Standing or hanging
Like the strokes of Hebrew letters
Marching in file
Moving across parchment
Across the pitted Arabia of Iowa field.

Withering stalks composed themselves,
Blackened with the smut of summer,
Corn of Egypt to be gathered.

The strangers kept in rented rooms
And learned their lines.

O radiant zero,
Whited barrows of odorous soil,
O lidless dome!

To an Elder

I certainly do
hand it to you
the fine vertical stricture
     of a machine's
tape. I tried
many ways to coax
the baby to walk.
Meters, regular footage
thumping away, carriage
wheels over Connecticut.

The form would appear
like a sprout
     from the black earth
and I might all night watch
     and catch
a glimpse of where I stood. Crutch
or structure
     it would do except
I didn't bring along a roll
and so the tape had to be
     imagined.

The form *would* appear,
a loosened song, free
furl, through which
night vision and
sidelong longing I
might catch direction out

a glimpse a
flicker—one moment through
one chink—lighting ways
                out and down
from nightwatch. Listen
        to the wind!
                        You have,
and have been
blessedly taking it
down half a life
                and I
think of the waiting
on it, Southern years,
        till finally
the sweep came through
would take care of itself
as the old moon like a tarnished
mirror rides
        in the arms of the new.

Thanksgiving Over the Water

The master cylinder of my cherished new
Secondhand Valiant is leaking.
My pedal goes to the floor already,

The slave cylinders do not respond, an ordinary
Experience obtained by ordinary
Commercial transaction. I am justified

If after paying for a replacement I feel
That this experience has not been real
Enough. And I may turn

To ordinary experience on a higher plane. The rain
Is gleaming on the slates
Of the barn where through a mist a wave

Of evening is falling, brightening
The thin, smooth stones. This brings me
Less complicated thoughts, notions

Perhaps archaic on this modern evening, modes
Of conceiving the effects of time
On space. Beauty is difficult, said Beardsley

Whose brief life and anguish in furnished parlors
Made him belong to a becoming
In which he found himself to be

Not himself. I think of the sculptor,
My friend, whose otherworldly metal
Intensities kept on when his strong hand

Began to turn, quelled in an ill wind;
Who never spoke the trying, holding
Pieces together; and watched the fields gone to scrub,

For everything changes to something else. The barn
That once held animals and hay
Yet houses lively creatures, and hay,

Though creatures a thousand times smaller, the hay
Too rotten to use except as mulch;
Just now, the haunt of bees: my barn

Stands brooding, stalled like an arthritic
Dinosaur in the rain. Over against this
Dry husk, dry under the hammered lapping

Of protecting slates and rafters, wings
Of carefully feathered stones, is a world
Which is not timeless so, if such a rhythmic

Pattern in the oiled, after-shower light may be
Considered timeless; or merely a figure
Of order that gleams beyond reckoning;

Beyond one's clocks and cruxes—beyond
Or in the foreground, other world
Where all is, always, of the moment.

Similarly the illusion of space with limits
Withers in loping fences, falling
Boundary markers lost whether ledge or cherry,

Rectangular fields eroded by curling waves
Of vegetation with 'other plans,' a surf
Of sumac, white pine, aspen; and I am grateful

For circuits of *there* becoming *here,* the precise
Area, say, of the blue surface of a car
Contained for a minute by a focus of consciousness,

The blue surface of a blue car then slowly
Going to brown, running to earth, the sky
Where it touches down as pools underfoot; as if smoke

In a rut of rainwater; dimples of rust, rising
Bursting the surface calm of the blue as blisters,
Golden atolls that never sleep: at the center

Of the illusion, the moving waters, the reward.

Adagio for Strings

Do not give me
The laces of Osiris, one
Summer of happiness,
The fine calves of Icarus

Dangling,
I am enough
With my little boat
Under the willow

Ready to cast off
Ready
To move up close to my life
Paddle along beside it

Ready to listen
To the hitches, the tease;
Going along abreast
Turning toward my days with a sly

Smile and saying
Softly, "Brother!
Here I am,
Brother."

Great Plains Dooryard

Here bricks are so rare they are like agates
We wonder who would carry them so far
Here he feels good because he has nothing
He is thinking about
Or that anyone would steal
He has no status but this doesn't matter
It matters that no one can tell him why though.

When he walks home to the plain board parlor
He is content that someone he loves
Needs to be cared for or nursed for a long time
And the bricks piled by the door are like cocoons
Each one bends a little
Arches ever so slightly.

She is already in the room and safe
Though there was no buggy not even a horse
It is a strange light she brings him
A kind of sodium splendor over the barnish dark
All manner of thing will be well
But he must not care how it appears.

Once bricks were everywhere
In the sky and underfoot
That was grandfather's world
They were legion they were unnoticed
Thinking about a brick was like trying to know death
But here they are so rare they are like agates
We wonder what carried them so far.

Fort Burial

The boy was eight and came running
From the box elder woods; he cried, "Hey, Dad,
You want to help me organize
    A mole funeral?"
The sun was going. I said I would,
Sure thing, as soon as I stopped raking.
He waited; then—he disappeared.
    I found him inside
In the kitchen, on his mother's lap
In tears. He stood then, thinking; some tears,
But thinking, mostly, about the dead;
    A proper burial
Of the mole. For coffin he chose a box
Blank checks had come in; a winding sheet
Of tissue; to garnish the lid a sprig
    Of bittersweet:
Long mole, plump prodigal, with pelt
Of midnight-glossy fur, like a ruff
Engraved by Hollar, clenched coral feet
    With Meissen claws
Minute, pink, and fragile-looking;
Yet ferocious in the power I felt
They barely now had given up,
    A moonless drudge
Whose silken frame meant business only.
My son considered it on its bier,
Stroked the fur sweet to him now
    As his stuffed toys.

Fort Burial

I fetched the spade; we buried it
By the edge of the field in a clump of sumac,
A bower the boy had named *the fort.*
    He found a crate slat
To mark the grave: with a nail on the pine
He scribed a legend: "In this Hole
Lies my Mole." Mercy, he
    Inscribed the grave!
He scored the words in deep—and smiled.
In half a twilight hour he
Had tried the work of mourning on;
    A death for the heart.

Mammal Pavilion

On a day in August with his children went
To the aquarium. Joined the serpent of zealous
Children advancing into the Floating Marine
Mammal Pavilion. Marching in place to the tune
Of dolphins trained, and one accomplished sea lion.
The canned mood music deafened; Bottlenosed Dolphins
Roiled their tank like hyperactive youngsters.
He did enjoy watching their bodies gleam
Like Royal Copenhagen porcelain under
The arc lights, breaching the sea slosh with prancing tumult,
Rising—sudden under the glare—walking
On water! They hurtled as if they played a sea-calm
Instead of toiling in the vise as now
Of music and a crowd. Before their work began
They swam as if alone, playing dolphin games;
Saving a shipwrecked boy, hoisting him high
To ride unharmed to the warm curve of land.

*

The sea lion knows what he will do,
He'll do just what we tell him to.
He'll cruise, or limp, or hurtle through
His paces; will, if asked, halloo—
As if across some acreage of sea
Bellowing his leonine degree.
Without a foot he stands upon
His tiny stool, a paragon
Of balance and mammalian grace!

Mammal Pavilion

A flipper-stand is commonplace,
Although at clapping he's not apt.
In fact, the beast is handicapped.
When we consider all the tasks
He does when his stern master asks,
And watching the one long thew he is,
It's wonderful he's such a whizz.
The one reward that goes to him
Is herring, at his master's whim,
But Pico doesn't give an inch.
He doesn't laugh or cry or flinch;
Ignores the children in the bleachers,
The tourist's flash, the science teachers.
Alone in his midnight, marbly pelf
He dreams of a day he'll find himself
Sniffing the breeze along the gleaming
Foreshore of a rockbound bay,
Hailing his lioness, the screaming
Of the screaming children washed away.

*

The house lights dim. A screen rolls down to show
A film clip of the whales, slow blameless swimmers
Cruising the booming shores of silence, through
Endless hangars of salt cold, illumined
Beneath the frosted pane of wimpling glass
The surface of the sea is when we view it
From below, the sky whales know before the other
Sky. Calling and wailing they keep their rounds,
Fraught codes inaudible to human ears;
Especially inaudible above
The sermonizing cello strains, a fulsome

Sound track to impress us. As a final treat
We overhear the whales, those bloky Nereids,
Singing each to each—a vacationing
Technologist has caught their eclogues on
A disc, like the passionate machinist who
Collects axe-heads, arrowheads, celts. Always
The whales are passing into deeps off camera,
Recede down rearranging halls of ocean.
Darkly they turn from us; resist their doom.

*

Three dolphins churn the un-Olympic pool—
Too small, watery socket—like a vase
With a bouquet of fins, white spray, black eyes.
High time: the trainer and her guards come on,
Laden with mikes; they put them to their tricks.
It is surprising, somehow, that they have names.
This one is Dixie, that one Rainbow, the third
Is Mack. Terrifying volumes of the music
Fill every aisle and wavelet; seem to rise
Whenever the trainer bellows out commands—
Or praise—to the dolphin trio. Rainbow is told
To let a member of the audience approach;
And kneel; and touch his crown, a tender place
And private, to judge from how the vigilant skin
Winces and the shining body draws back toward
Its element. It is a laying on of hands,
Another way around; a blessing in reverse.
I see that places on a dolphin all
Are private; and sensitive, touching as dolphins do
No more than the old oceans streaming by;
Flesh sensitive as ears, those dolphins ears—

How finely tuned! The trainer is shouting to us
Over the echoes from applause. I watch them being
Dolphins—make soggy tickets do for ear plugs—
And wipe the sea spray from my face, enthralled.

On the Street

Sometimes, thinking of you eaten by absence,
When the square whitens with shoots of spiraea,
The sun mercuric on ouzo and water,
I stand on the steps with desire.

When the square whitens with shoots of spiraea
A whiff of exhaust smudges the air;
I stand on the steps with desire
Taking comfort in an earth which is powerless.

A whiff of exhaust smudges the air
Past the window in flower, the flowery walk.
Taking comfort in an earth which is powerless
I want to do the right thing, I want to go back

Past the window in flower, the flowery walk.
Forgetting the broken key of your face
I want to do the right thing, I want to go back
And see the day through desire.

Forgetting the broken key of your face
I stand on the steps in the licorice sun
And see the day through desire
Watching the boys on the square play touch.

I stand on the steps in the licorice sun
Sometimes, thinking of you eaten by absence,
Watching the boys on the square play touch,
The sun mercuric on ouzo and water.

Around Our Table

For Stephen Fels, 1940–1989

He was coming out of the dark
To join us at our picnic table,
He was about to head back down
The thin corridors of waiting.
He might have cried, "I don't need Belsen,
I have my body." Instead he called,
"You may not recognize me, I
Am Stephen. I came to see you anyway."
But right away I knew the bones,
A quiet incandescence in our midst,
His face in a glow like a straining runner's
In the little light our candles made.

You who came through the August dark,
Who came to us without your hair,
Without color, scarcely with flesh,
You walked around the corner to us
And cried "hello there" in the dark;
Before we could see, you called our names.
"You are Geoffrey, you are James,
You're Kate." We did not know how joy
And fear could come together so
As one; in the unfeeling breeze
Of the unspeakable, your bright face
Like a lamp in the dark around our table.

And that was something, as one who finds
His father, years perhaps beyond
His death, in subway or crowded street,
A presence felt that may tell something
Or tell nothing, some commission
Or timely caution from beyond
The grave, or maybe none; one who
In his devotion plays the fool
And fails to comprehend, just yet,
What he must do. Stephen, you were
The message we waited for, glowing face
Like a lamp in the dark around our table.

Mother's Day

Back from the round of visits, I take
The straight-edge spade and the steel rake
And start by cutting in and slicing under
The turf, lifting the pared squares.
Heaving rectangles, triangles, odd
Clumps of green earth-skin away
To plant a tree here, add grass there;
Trundling loads in the wheelbarrow
Around back, fitting them in again,
Tucking them back (friable selvage
Of drying root-strung loam pellets,
Dribble from earthen soffits, hanging
Like bangles from Grendel's necklace). I push
And pat, snugging them close together
As if bedding bricks up in mortar
At the spread and slap of the trowel, kneading
The roughly sifted dirt in, pulling
Sinewy taproots of dandelion,
The insidious net of bittersweet fuse
Snaking in the hush of soil to blossom;
Then the tamping down with booted feet,
Lightly springing my body, lightly
Beating earth with an easy measure;
Connecting the hose with rusty couplings
Stiff from winter, washers brittle
Or gone altogether, slobbering; then
Hosing the ground, soaking the sods that look
As if pleased to be hugging earth again

—Heavy they lie, pressing warm dirt!—
Letting the water play over the sods,
Washing them green, sogging them in.
Now while the streams are mingling over
The mosaic of living pieces knit up
In a strange bed, clods no more aware
Of where they once were than where they are,
Indistinguishable in a week from grass
They're bedded next to, now I watch
The new flies gather for their first rally
Of the season, swarm on the rim of the blue
Wheelbarrow. There at the hedgerow, under
The maple sprouts making ready to leaf
But still gray sticks in the gray ground
I watch ajuga, hosta, fiddleheads coming,
Taking tentative looks at the new world;
And hear the redwings calling, and the robins;
Strange: after drear dark the strange, sweet
Business of the birds overhead once more.

Stephen Sandy is the author of five previous collections of poems, including *Riding to Greylock* (1983) and *Man in the Open Air* (1988). He has taught at Harvard, Brown, The University of Tokyo, Tokyo University of Foreign Studies, the University of Rhode Island, and Bennington College. His honors include fellowships from the National Endowment for the Arts, the Ingram Merrill Foundation, the Vermont Council on the Arts and a Fulbright Lectureship in Japan. He lives with his family in Vermont.

A NOTE ON THE TYPE

This book is set in a film version of a typeface called PERPETUA, designed by Eric Gill at the suggestion of Stanley Morison in his capacity as typographical adviser to the Monotype Corporation in London. Stanley Morison (1889–1967) was a type designer in his own right, and in Times Roman he produced one of the most famous and influential typefaces of the twentieth century. As adviser to Monotype he commissioned a dozen faces of the highest quality from a distinguished group of which Gill was one. Eric Gill (1882–1940) cast his net wide as a designer and artist, and had achieved an international reputation as a master in letter cutting in stone, which led to this commission. After a period of some years, in which trial cuttings were made by Charles Malin of Paris from Gill's original drawings, the face made its first appearance in 1929 in Gill's own book, *Art-Nonsense*. Originally the roman was known as Perpetua, and the italic, which followed, was named Felicity; honoring two early Christians martyred at Carthage in the year 203.

Composition by Creative Graphics Inc., Allentown, Pennsylvania
Printing and binding by Halliday Lithographers,
West Hanover, Massachusetts
Designed by Harry Ford